Overtime Pay Practices for Exempt Employees

THE CONFERENCE BOARD

ABOUT THE CONFERENCE BOARD

The Conference Board is an independent, not-for-profit research institution with facilities in the United States, Canada and Europe. Its scientific studies of management and economics produce a continuing flow of timely and practical information to assist leaders of business, government, labor and other institutions in arriving at sound decisions. The Board's research is also made available to the news media in order to contribute to public understanding of economic and management issues in market economies.

Worldwide, The Conference Board is supported financially by more than 4,000 Associates, comprised of corporations, national and regional governments, labor unions, universities, associations, public libraries and individuals.

THE BOARD'S SERVICES

Research reports, personalized information services and access to a variety of meetings are among the direct benefits that Associates receive from The Conference Board. Associate Relations representatives at the address listed below will describe these activities in detail and will tailor delivery of Board services to the specific needs of Associate organizations. Inquiries from locations other than in Canada and Europe should be addressed to The Conference Board, Inc. in New York.

The Conference Board, Inc.
845 Third Avenue, New York, New York 10022
(212) 759-0900
Telex: 234465 and 237282

The Conference Board in Canada
Suite 100, 25 McArthur Road, Ottawa, Ontario K1L-6R3
(613) 746-1261

The Conference Board in Europe
Avenue Louise, 207 Bte 5, B-1050 Brussels, Belgium
(02) 640 62 40
Telex: 63635

Conference Board Report No. 797   Printed In U.S.A.

ISBN No.: 0-8237-0233-2

Overtime Pay Practices for Exempt Employees

by Burton W. Teague

A Research Report from The Conference Board

Contents

Tables

About This Report

THIS REPORT DESCRIBES the prevalence of overtime pay plans for employees exempt from the provisions of the Fair Labor Standards Act in just under 1,000 firms in the manufacturing, utility, insurance, banking, construction and retail industries. It shows how the adoption or rejection of such plans may be influenced by company characteristics such as size and industry. The plans are analyzed to reflect their rationale, the levels of exempt employees included, the hours of overtime considered compensable, and the rates applied.

In reaching a decision to compensate employees for overtime if they are exempt under the provisions of the Fair Labor Standards Act (1938, as amended almost annually) and the Walsh-Healey Act of 1938 (relating to public contracts) executives are faced with a problem of resolving a conflict between compensation theory and economic reality. In theory supervisory employees are paid to get the job done, not for the hours it takes them to do it.

But the pressure of inflation, production schedules, trade-offs in costs, and the compression in salary scales due to rapidly increasing rates of pay for labor may be sufficient to overcome the reluctance to treat exempt staff in the same manner as those who are nonexempt.

Prevalence

Nearly half of the nearly 1,000 firms surveyed for this study do compensate exempt personnel for overtime in some manner. The practice is most common among manufacturers and utility companies (63 percent and 65 percent respectively); and it is least common among retailing companies and insurance firms (both 27 percent). But the practice is growing in all industrial lines.

The practice is most common among the firms employing large numbers of employees—above 5,000.

Only a small number of companies limit overtime pay to compensating equivalent time off (15 percent), but half of the retailers and 35 percent of the insurance companies follow this practice.

Control

Companies control exempt overtime by sharply defining eligibility—setting organizational limits; salary limits; specifying what constitutes overtime; prohibiting payment for casual, voluntary and customary overtime; limiting compensable overtime to those hours when nonexempt personnel are also required to work; requiring prior executive approval of the extra time; and controlling (by setting limits to the overtime premium) the total amount of overtime pay per day week, month or quarter.

Method

About half of the firms surveyed prefer the simplicity of the straight-time overtime compensation plan for exempt personnel. A few firms make it even simpler by paying a flat dollar amount—either in lump sum, for the day or shift, or by the hour. Some have developed "formulas" for compensating exempts for overtime. Some of the plans are progressive, paying higher premiums for longer periods of overtime, while other formulas are regressive, paying less premium to higher paid employees. A few state their premiums in terms of percent of base weekly or monthly salary, lowering the percent as the salary levels increase.

Weekends and Holidays

A few firms pay only when weekend or holiday overtime is involved. The largest number of firms pay straight time for Saturdays, Sundays and holidays. They are followed closely, however, by the number of firms that pay 1.5 times the base rate for those overtime workdays. And a significant number of firms pay 1.5 times for Saturday work; double time for Sundays and holidays.

The Trend

Despite the fact that this survey was conducted in the midst of a sharp recession, most firms reported either a fairly constant amount of exempt overtime or a slight increase. Though productivity may have fallen during the period, the requirements for information did not; and the paperwork load remains or even increases during business cycle bottoms. This load falls most heavily on supervisors and other administrative personnel.

It is not surprising, then, that the largest proportion of the plans in existence (among respondents to this survey) have been adopted since 1974. The majority of these show a preference for the straight-time rate of compensation (no premium). The majority of the plans adopted prior to 1965 show a preference for the 1.5 times base method.

The wide variety of plans in effect, explained only in part by industry and company differences, suggests that while the practice of paying for overtime worked by exempt personnel is growing steadily, it is also still evolving. At this stage of the "state of the art" it cannot be accused of uniformity.

Foreword

IN MAKING ANY POLICY DECISION, management attempts to achieve a dynamic balance between theory and pragmatics, between pressures and sound practice. One of the questions management has had to consider for a long time is whether or not to pay exempt personnel for the extra hours of work they perform in overtime.

The laws governing the payment of overtime specifically exclude and exempt executives, professional and administrative employees; yet nearly half of the companies in this study of nearly 1,000 firms do pay many groups of such employees in order to maintain a satisfactory differential in the compensation between them and the employees they direct. This report examines the reasons for those decisions and considers the details of the compensation plans related to the practice.

The Conference Board gratefully acknowledges the cooperation of the executives who provided data for their companies' plans. The author also wishes to express his gratitude to D.A. Weeks Jr., of Vanderbilt University, for his assistance in the collection, tabulation and analysis of the data upon which this report is based.

KENNETH A. RANDALL
President

Chapter 1
Overtime and the Exempt Employee

IN REACHING A DECISION to compensate employees who are exempt from the provisions of the Fair Labor Standards Act and the Walsh-Healey Act, executives are faced with the problem of resolving a conflict between compensation theory and economic reality. In theory, supervisory pay scales are set at levels sufficiently above those of production and clerical workers they direct to compensate them adequately for the added responsibility and such reasonable overtime as may be necessary. And, at least in theory, they are paid for getting the job done, not for the hours they may work. Again in theory, if significant amounts of overtime are required by a supervisor, either the work unit he or she directs is understaffed or that supervisor is not planning the work correctly.

As a practical matter, neither theory covers most overtime situations. No company wants to staff every unit to the maximum for peak production periods. The cost prohibits it. No planner can anticipate every emergency either. Yet peak loads and emergencies occur in every business with regular irregularity. "What do you tell a supervisor when for the past several months a number of his employees' take-home pay has exceeded his or hers? What explanation can we give to professional and technical personnel when we have to schedule four weekends of work in succession, one including a holiday?"

There has been a dramatic increase in questions such as these that are addressed to The Conference Board by personnel executives across American industry. In the past, most companies have been satisfied to grant compensatory time off to exempt personnel when they have been called upon to work significant amounts of overtime. But this practice has a serious drawback—it compounds the overtime problem. Time off means that regular work may fall behind, requiring more overtime later. On the production line, it may mean another foreman is needed to replace the one taking time off.

1

Who Is Exempt?

As a reminder of the legal provisions that can serve as a guide for determining the exempt status of executive and administrative personnel under the wage and hour laws, the following short-form tests may be kept in mind. Each of these "tests" depends on the employee being guaranteed a minimum earnings level (amended from time to time—now $155, exclusive of board, lodging and other facilities awarded by the employer). And, not more than 20 percent of the hours in a workweek may be spent on activities not directly related to executive, administrative or professional functions.

With those limitations in mind:

An executive may be exempt if his or her function is that of managing the enterprise or a division of it, and the person customarily directs the work of two or more employees;

An administrative employee may be exempt if he or she performs work requiring the consistent exercise of discretion and judgment and the individual performs nonmanual office work relating to management policies or general business operations;

A professional employee may be exempt if his or her primary duties require knowledge of an advanced type in a recognized science that requires professional levels of learning and the work requires consistent exercise of discretion and judgment, or he or she works in a recognized field of artistic endeavor involving imagination, talent or invention.

In short, all three exemptions are related to intellectual work, varied in character, that cannot be standardized or related to being performed within a specific period of time.

The so-called "short-form test"—$250 per week of income—can be a trap. While it is true that executive, administrative and professional employees whose salaries are at or above that level are almost certainly exempt, many nonexempt persons may also earn at that level. Any question relating to exemption under the wage-hour laws should be referred to counsel.

Another economic reality—in companies with organized bargaining units, labor-management agreements calling for 30 percent increases over 2.5 to 3 years are not uncommon. The federal guidelines of the Council for Wage and Price Stability for merit increases to exempt personnel are considerably below that. Some companies have found that this has created a compression in their pay scales for exempt employees which can be at least partly offset by extending their overtime plans to supervisors. And many companies are now restudying their overtime plans, some believing the practice might now be curtailed in the light of the current recession (many of the plans were extended to exempts during the red-hot 1960's), and others believing that the compression of pay scales exerted by much higher union rates, especially in the central cities, may have forced the practice on them.

To help answer the questions of personnel executives and to provide compensation planners with some hard data on the subject, The Conference Board surveyed 932 companies in the manufacturing, utility, insurance, banking, retail and construction industries to determine whether there has been an increase or decrease in the number of companies paying overtime to exempt staff, to find out to whom the overtime pay is granted, how the plans work, and the rationale if not adopted or extended to exempt personnel.

In summary, the answers are:

• The Conference Board conducted two prior studies of this subject, one in 1959 and the second in 1967, both periods of high industrial and commercial activity, when overtime work was essential to meet unprecedented demand in many quarters. The present study was conducted during a sharp recession. Despite this, far more companies report that exempt overtime has remained fairly constant (or has increased in the recent past) than report a decline in exempt overtime.

• The sample of companies in the last two surveys are not identical. The 1967 survey covered 673 companies, the current survey covers 932 companies. Generally, the broader the sample, the lower the percentage of companies that have adopted the practice being studied. The reverse occurred in this instance—another indication of a rising trend. (The current survey indicates a 12 percent rise in the number of exempt overtime pay plans). Another indication—the largest number of plans have been adopted since 1965 and most of those since 1974.

• A company's size and geographic dispersion around the United States is a factor determining the adoption or rejection of an overtime plan for exempt staff. The larger the company the more likely it is to have such a plan, although the plan may be unevenly applied locally, depending on local practice.

• The majority of the plans in effect provide for cash compensation rather than equivalent time off with pay; and a significant percentage pay a premium for overtime worked by exempt personnel.

• About three-quarters of the plans include engineers, technicians, professional workers, and middle managers; moreover, the largest percentage have a high cut-off salary limit ($30,000 and up).

It is evident from this survey that the practice of paying overtime to exempt personnel is growing and being extended. But it is also evident that the policy is still evolving. There is little uniformity in the practice. Companies are still struggling with the conflict between theory and reality.

3

Take the insurance industry as an example. The majority of the plans in that industry are fairly new. The reason is the need to accommodate the influx of professional and technical personnel to operate the computers on which they rely. Technicians, especially supervisory technicians, are in seriously short supply in the profession. And the velocity with which computer technology is changing is mind-boggling. Change-overs and reprogramming are becoming routine. This means overtime and lots of it. Technicians tend to be more easily wooed away with higher salary offers today than in the past. Loyalty to one's profession has replaced loyalty to one's company to a marked extent. A company that cannot keep pace with the compensation demands of its technical staff is bound to lose valuable staff. Hence, the overtime pay plan for these people.

The Pros and Cons

Although the trend is clearly in the direction of paying exempt personnel for overtime worked, and the large majority in many industries do, industrywide, slightly more than half do not. The reasons that about half do and a bit more than half do not are both pragmatic. Costs—or the reduction of costs—figure in the arguments on both sides. Pressures from employees, staff shortages, and the economic realities of inflation are perceived differently by different companies in different industries. The reasons *for* and *aganst* adopting and applying overtime pay plans for exempt employees are discussed below.

Reasons For

• Sustained, rather than occasional, overtime has become a fairly constant problem in some departments in some companies and industries despite lower plant productivity during this recent period. While plant output may have decreased, the administrative work has not; indeed, it has increased in some respects. The added work load tends to fall on supervisors and technical people. "We still have to make reports (often more of them) to management and government agencies."

• Inflation and union pressures combine to bring compressions to exempt salary levels, especially in central cities where wage rates for the hourly and weekly paid production workers have skyrocketed.

• "Shortages of good technical people force us to give them ample consideration whenever feasible."

• If equity is to be preserved in the pay scales, overtime pay for exempts is a necessity at the lower levels. The differential between the worker and his or her immediate supervisor is rapidly disappearing because of inflation, union pressures and the federal guideline on merit increases. A foreman should earn, say, 20 percent more than the most highly paid worker in the group. If a worker is paid $4 per hour, he would receive $160 for a 40 hour week, but his or her supervisor should then get $200 for the week. If the

Table 1: Reasons for NOT Paying Overtime to Exempt Employees (465 Companies)

Reason	Manufacturing (N = 134)		Banks (N = 133)		Insurance (N = 105)		Retail (N = 43)		Utility (N = 26)		Construction (N = 24)		Companies (N = 465)	
	Number	Percent	Number	Percent	Number	Percent	Number	Percent	Number	Percent	Number	Percent	Number	Percent
Exempt pay is structured to compensate for reasonable overtime....	102	76%	96	72%	65	62%	36	84%	25	96%	14	58%	338	73%
There is no problem in maintaining a differential between exempt and nonexempt total pay....	43	32	59	44	51	49	19	44	5	19	9	38	186	40
Exempt employees rarely work significant amounts of overtime....	15	11	40	30	27	26	8	19	5	19	8	33	103	22

supervisor is not paid overtime and the worker must be paid time-and-one-half, the differential will disappear with one Saturday shift (40 x $4 + 8 x $6 = $208). It is cheaper for the company to pay the supervisor overtime than it is to increase his or her base rate always to exceed the total take-home pay of the workers supervised.

• A certain amount of overtime is considered when supervisory salaries are set in the scale; but if management schedules sustained overtime the equation has to be amended.

• Equivalent time off with pay is no answer. It eventually pyramids the overtime problem.

• Paying overtime avoids the added cost of increased base salary granted to preserve differentials.

Reasons Against

• The vast majority of companies that do not extend their overtime pay plans to exempt personnel state that exempt pay levels are structured to provide compensation for a reasonable amount of overtime.

• Somewhat under half of the same companies state that they have had no difficulty in maintaining appropriate differentials between exempt and nonexempt pay levels.

• And, about one-quarter of those companies state their exempt personnel rarely work significant amounts of overtime.

Those replies and differences between industries are reflected in Table 1.

Chapter 2
Prevalence of Exempt Overtime Pay

WELL OVER HALF of the manufacturing and utility companies surveyed pay one or more classes of exempt employees for overtime hours worked. In the construction industry it is about half, but the practice is far less prevalent among banking, retail and insurance companies (see Table 2).

Differences between industries in this practice are striking, but more striking is the fact that as the number of a company's employees increases in all industries, the percentage that have overtime plans increases dramatically. For example, in the manufacturing industry about one-third of the companies employing less than 1,000 employees have overtime plans for exempts. But the percentage nearly doubles for those with over 1,000 employees. The same general pattern is followed in all six industries. Even in the retail line, which has the lowest aggregate percentage, over 40 percent of the large retailers follow the practice.

Whether this tendency in the large firms is due to fundamental policy differences, to the more complex demands of a large exempt work force, or to the likelihood of more formalized or sophisticated salary administration programs in large companies is open to conjecture. From the comments made about their programs by executives in these firms, it appears that all of those reasons are involved (see Table 3).

Most Exempt Pay Plans Are New

Of those companies that responded to the question of how long they had been compensating exempt employees for overtime worked, the majority had adopted their plans in the last six years. The next largest groups adopted their plans between the years 1965 to 1973; only about 10 percent adopted plans prior to 1965. From this, it is reasonable to conclude that the practice is growing significantly. (See Table 4.)

Table 2: Overtime Payments to Exempt Employees, by Type of Business

Type of Business	Total Companies		Companies That Pay Overtime	
	Number	Percent	Number	Percent
Manufacturing	390		245	63%
Utilities	77		50	65
Banks	211		69	33
Insurance	144		39	27
Retail.	59		16	27
Construction.	51		24	47
Total	932		443	48%

This trend is more pronounced in the nonmanufacturing industries.

It may be noted that the 1967 survey by The Conference Board of 172 manufacturing companies suggested just the opposite conclusion.[1] This apparent discrepancy is explained by the fact that two additional industries have been added to this survey, retail and construction, in both of which the practice of paying overtime to exempt personnel has been recently growing. It has also been recently favored by the banking and insurance lines, due largely to the influx of large numbers of computer technicians.

Industry Differences

So far all manufacturing companies in this report have been grouped together in comparison with the other five types of business surveyed. While the overtime problems of the others are reasonably similar within each, this is not true of all manufacturing companies. Durable goods manufacturers differ from consumer product manufacturers, and within each of these groups there are different problems and different responses to those problems, as Table 5 reflects.

Overtime plans are in effect for exempt employees in 72 percent of the industrial goods manufacturing companies, but in only 52 percent of the consumer goods manufacturers—a difference of 20 percent.

The most likely explanation for this difference can be found in the cyclical nature of business in the ten industrial groupings. It is probable that the incidence of overtime in cyclical industries during periods of high

[1]David A. Weeks, *Overtime Pay for Exempt Employees*. The National Industrial Conference Board, Personnel Policy Study No. 208, 1967.

8

Table 3: Overtime Payments to Exempt Employees, by Size of Company, by Industry

Total Employment	Manufacturing			Utilities			Banks and Insurance		
	Total Companies	Companies Paying	Percent	Total Companies	Companies Paying	Percent	Total Companies	Companies Paying	Percent
20,000 + ...	84	62	74%	1	1	100%	3	1	33%
10,000—19,999...	67	40	60	9	9	100	7	4	57
5,000— 9,999...	72	42	58	15	13	87	16	10	63
2,500— 4,999...	84	58	69	21	15	71	30	16	53
1,000— 2,499...	51	31	61	25	10	40	82	28	34
Under 1,000.......	19	7	37	6	2	33	207	45	22
Not specified	13	5	39	—	—	—	10	4	40

Table 3: Overtime Payments to Exempt Employees, by Size of Company, by Industry (continued)

Total Employment	Retail			Construction		
	Total Companies	Companies Paying	Percent	Total Companies	Companies Paying	Percent
20,000 + ...	12	5	42%	2	2	100%
10,000—19,999...	7	2	29	2	2	100
5,000— 9,999...	14	4	29	2	2	100
2,500— 4,999...	11	3	27	6	3	50
1,000— 2,499...	11	2	18	17	8	47
Under 1,000.......	4	—	0	19	5	26
Not specified	—	—	—	3	2	66

Table 4: When Overtime Plans for Exempt Employees Were Adopted

Date Adopted			Manufacturing		Nonmanufacturing	
	Number of Companies	Percent	Number of Companies	Percent	Number of Companies	Percent
1974-80	115	51%	54	35%	61	58%
1965-73	86	38%	54	35%	32	30%
Prior to 1965 .	25	11%	47	30%	13	12%
	226	100%	155	100%	106	100%

Table 5: Differences Between Manufacturing Industries

Industry Class	Number of Companies Surveyed	Number Paying Overtime	Within Each Group, Percent Paying Overtime
Industrial			
Rubber...........................	5	4	80%
Diversified.......................	18	10	56
Primary and Fabricated Metals	30	19	63
Transportation Equipment	15	13	87
Machinery........................	15	13	87
Electric Machinery and Electronics....	28	23	82
Building Materials	15	10	67
Miscellaneous	54	38	70
Total	180	130	72%
Consumer Goods			
Consumer Chemicals	30	16	53%
Food and Tobacco..................	33	17	52
Paper and Printing.................	30	16	53
Glass............................	4	3	75
Toys.............................	3	2	67
Textiles and Apparel	15	8	53
Consumer Durables.................	11	6	55
Petroleum and Energy...............	13	2	15[a]
General	6	5	83
Total	145	75	52%

[a]Petroleum and energy companies pay high wages and have a conservative bias against paying supervisors for overtime.

Table 6: Companies Granting Only Compensatory Time Off, by Type of Business

Industry Group	Number of Companies with Overtime Plans	Number of Companies Time Off Only	Percent Time Off Only
Retail	16	8	50%
Banks and Insurance	108	38	35
Construction	24	3	13
Manufacturing.......................	245	16	7
Utilities............................	50	1	2
Total	443	66	15%

productivity has forced a larger percentage of companies in that group to adopt policies for compensating exempts, and that such policies remain in effect during recessionary periods as well.

Compensatory Time Off—Only

A small percentage of the companies surveyed that have overtime pay plans for exempt personnel provide compensatory time off *ONLY* (15 percent). This practice is most prevalent in the retail industry (50 percent and among the banks and insurance companies (35 percent). It is almost nonexistent in the manufacturing and utilities industries, as Table 6 reflects.

Chapter 3
Problems of Eligibility and Control

A_{LMOST} ALL OF THE COMPANIES use a combination of eligibility
rules and administrative provisions to limit their obligation for overtime
pay and the increased costs that accompany it.

Two basic approaches are used to limit and control overtime of exempt
employees: First, certain groups of exempt employees may be declared
ineligible, either because of the nature and level of their managerial
positions, or because their salaries exceed certain specified levels. This is
sometimes accomplished by one specific guideline; at other times it is applied in gradual steps. Second, both direct and indirect controls are set up
by defining the hours of work that are considered compensable. A further
control is usually applied by requiring prior managerial approval of the
extra working time.

Which Exempt Employees Are Eligible?

Most of the literature relating to overtime payments to exempt employees
stresses that an important purpose of such plans is to maintain an optimum
salary differential between production foremen and workers. Wage and
salary administrators generally agree that establishing or ensuring such a
differential is a valid reason for making overtime payments to line supervisors.

But focusing on this one level of exempt employees tends to obscure the
fact that the majority of companies pay overtime to other groups of exempt
personnel as well. Most include professional and technical employees, many
include "middle management," and some have no organizational breaking
point at all (although overtime payments to top management are rare, if
they exist at all).

Table 7 shows the patterns of overtime payments to the seven different
levels and groups of exempt employees in 443 plans studied in the six industries surveyed. (Banks and insurance companies are grouped together in
this instance because of the similarity of the employees they engage and the

12

Table 7: Level of Exempt Employee Paid for Overtime, by Industry

Level of Exempt Employee	Manufacturing (N = 245)		Utility (N = 50)		Banks and Insurance (N = 108)		Retail (N = 16)		Construction (N = 24)		Total Companies (N = 443)	
	Number	Percent	Number	Percent	Number	Percent	Number	Percent	Number	Percent	Number	Percent
Plant First-Line Supervisors	213	87%	47	94%	2	2%	4	25%	5	21%	271	61%
Clerical First-Line Supervisors	100	41	24	48	49	45	3	19	5	21	181	41
Plant Middle Management	41	17	11	22	4	4	1	6	2	8	59	13
Clerical Exempt Employees	65	27	16	32	40	37	2	13	4	17	127	29
Professional and Technical	92	38	28	56	57	53	6	38	12	50	195	44
Office Middle Management	36	15	22	44	26	24	2	13	10	42	96	22
Upper Management	3	1	—	—	4	4	—	—	2	8	9	2

Table 8: Paid Overtime—Organizational Limits (by percentage)

Type of Business	Number of Companies	First-Line Supervisor	Second-Third Supervisor	Department-Head Assistant Manager	No Limit	Not Specified
Utility	49	25%	4%	24%	31%	16%
Retail.........	9	33	0	45	11	11
Construction ..	21	0	4	57	29	10
Banking	41	5	0	63	32	0
Insurance	28	4	0	46	43	7
Manufacturing .	216	38	5	20	25	12
All	364	28%	4%	30%	27%	11%

activities in which they are engaged). Table 8 shows the top organizational limits set by 364 companies in the six industries.

It will be noted that the manufacturing and utility companies cover their plant first-line supervisors to the greatest extent. Next in line are the professional and technical exempt staff, followed by clerical first-line supervisors and other clerical exempts. Office and plant middle management enjoy coverage in a significant percentage of the companies' plans as well. But most notable is the attention given to professional and technical exempt staff in all six industries. This might well be expected in the manufacturing, utility and construction industries. The attention they are now getting in the retail, banking and insurance industries reflects the degree to which computer technology has entered and become a significant factor in their business.

Some companies limit their overtime pay plans to specific groups or classes of exempt personnel. For example, almost one third of the manufacturing companies single out first-line supervisors only for this favorable treatment. Among banks and insurance companies, almost one-quarter of the plans are exclusively for the benefit of technical and professional staff, as are 40 percent of the plans of retail companies.

Eligibility and Salary Level

In addition to limiting participation in the overtime pay plan to clusters of exempt jobs classified by level of responsibility, 107 of the companies (24 percent) set maximum salary limits—employees whose salaries exceed those limits are not eligible for overtime pay under any circumstances (see Table 9). Although in total it is a minority practice, the salary limit concept is followed by a significant number of companies in each industry (manufacturing—30 percent; utilities—30 percent; banks and insurance— 12 percent; retail and construction each 13 percent). Among banks and insurance companies, as well as retail companies, the cut-off points are considerably lower than among manufacturing, utility and construction companies, as Table 9 reflects.

Some companies do not set specific salary or organizational limits but accomplish the same degree of control in a different manner. Some say there are no limits, but officers (or executives) are not included. Others say no overtime pay is granted to those employees who are eligible for payments under the bonus or profit-sharing plans. The assumption in both instances is that such exempt employees and executives are amply rewarded by any potential increase in the payout from the bonuses or shares, and the overtime they work is in the direction of increasing that payout.

What Are Overtime Hours Worked?

Another method of controlling overtime and its related costs is to define precisely what work is compensable as overtime. The five-day, forty-hour week is standard in the United States. Yet many companies now actually schedule 35, 37.5, even 38.25 hours. A few have set four-day workweeks. The general practice in a given industry and in the locale generally determines the actual schedule.

But each company has the further option of determining when overtime begins, and that may be beyond the normally scheduled workday or workweek. Since 40 hours is still the standard despite the growing practice of reducing it somewhat, many companies say that number of hours must be worked before overtime commences (as is the case for those employees covered by the Fair Labor Standards Act). In addition, many companies require an additional block of hours to be worked by exempt personnel before the time counts as compensable. The numbers of hours in those blocks vary, of course, but the numbers most often observed are 44 and 46 hours.

The justification most often heard for the added block of hours is that supervisors and professional people by the very nature of their assignments require some flexibility in their work time. Their jobs require something more than rigid adherence to the clock. A few hours of extra working time here and there are to be expected and are already compensated in the base salary.

A few companies adhere to the concept in the Walsh-Healey Act, which follows the "daily" overtime principle. Most companies calculate overtime for exempt employees on the basis of the workweek. Very few consider the time on a monthly or quarterly basis.

Some companies pay for overtime only on weekends and on holidays. These practices are reflected in Table 10. It will be noted that while the predominant approach is to pay for all overtime worked either above the normal workday or week, or the normally scheduled workweek, none of the practices enjoys a majority following.

Table 9: Maximum Salary Category Above Which Employees Are Ineligible for Overtime Payments (107 Companies)[a]

Maximum Salary	Manufacturing[b]		Utility		Banks and Insurance		Construction[b]		Retail		All Companies	
	Number	Percent	Number	Percent	Number	Percent	Number	Percent	Number	Percent	Number	Percent
$30,000 +	24	32%	12	80%	2	15%	2	66%	—	—	40	37%
$27,000-29,999	6	8	2	13	—	—	—	—	—	—	8	8
$25,000-26,999	9	12	—	—	2	15	—	33	—	—	11	10
$23,000-24,999	9	12	—	—	—	—	1	—	—	—	10	9
$20,000-22,999	3	4	—	—	1	8	—	—	—	—	4	4
Under $19,999	5	7	—	—	7	54	—	—	1	50%	13	12
Unspecified	18	24	1	7	1	8	—	—	1	50	21	20
Total	74	100%	15	100%	13	100%	3	100%	2	100%	107	100%

Note: a) Does not include those companies whose plans call for compensating time off only.
b) Percentages may not add to precisely 100% in all cases due to rounding.

Table 10: Overtime Hours Worked—Eligible for Payment, by Type of Business

Hours Worked In Excess	Manufacturing		Utility		Banks and Insurance		Construction		Retail		All Companies	
	Number	Percent	Number	Percent	Number	Percent	Number	Percent	Number	Percent	Number	Percent
All hours in excess of normal workday week	72	35%	18	44%	4	6%	6	32%	—	—	100	30%
All hours in excess of normal *scheduled* workday week	53	26	5	12	24	36	7	36	3	37%	92	27
All hours in excess of normally scheduled daily hours	21	10	6	15	2	3	2	11	—	—	31	9
All hours in excess of specified block of hours to be worked at no pay	30	15	6	15	19	28	2	11	1	13	58	17
Pay only for weekend and holiday overtime	3	2	—	—	2	3	—	—	1	13	6	2
Unspecified	24	12	6	14	16	24	2	10	3	37	51	15
Total	203	100%	41	100%	67	100%	19	100%	8	100%	338	100%

Note: Companies compensating by equivalent time off are not included.

17

Further Restrictions on Compensable Overtime

There are several other means of controlling overtime payments to exempt staff. Some are indirect controls exerted outside of the plans themselves, and some are provided for in the terms of written policies. In either case, the effect is the same: They prohibit counting overtime as compensable when it is casual, voluntary or customary. (See box for definitions.)

The majority of the companies in all industries have provisions in their overtime pay plans prohibiting compensation for casual or voluntary overtime. Over one-third of the companies do not permit customary overtime, but it is a standoff in the utilities industry and nearly one-half of

---

Company Definitions of Casual, Voluntary and Customary Overtime

"No restrictions are placed on the amount of time an exempt employee may voluntarily remain in the office for reading, studying, planning and so on, which the employee may consider desirable from an individual standpoint, but is not required in the performance of the work. Time spent in this manner is not considered compensable overtime."—*Life Insurance Company*

"The following are not considered hours worked toward normal hour quota and possible overtime pay:
(1) Time spent working on company business at home;
(2) Time spent at dinners and meetings at which attendance is voluntary;
(3) Standby time at home;
(4) Time required before or after a shiftchange to become acquainted with or to give information concerning the status of the job;
(5) Time before or after normal working hours for travel, to look after orders, make reports, secure materials, and so forth."—*Electric Utility*

"It is normal as part of some positions to work longer than the customary day to complete assignments and perform the duties and responsibilities of the job. Monetary reimbursement for such customary overtime may be made only when the exempt employee is working in a formally approved program or schedule."—*Manufacturer*

"Payments are not intended for occasional, casual or customary overtime—those hours arranged voluntarily on the exempt employee's own initiative—to complete his or her normal work."—*Pharmaceutical Manufacturer*

---

the companies in the manufacturing industries do prohibit payment for such overtime worked, as shown in Table 11.

While majority of companies do not pay exempt employees for voluntary, casual or customary overtime, (the latter is taken into account when the base rate for the job is set), a significant number of these go a step further and require that the the number of hours (per day or week) of work must be formally extended beyond the normal workday or week before an exempt employee will qualify for overtime payments. This is most common in the construction industry. Half of the companies surveyed in that industry follow that practice. Table 12 reflects the differences among industry groupings.

The differences between the industry groups may be explained by the fact that extended overtime is more easily anticipated in some than in others. For example, the lower incidence of the practice among utilities is due to fact that, in this industry, emergencies due to storms, local power outages caused by mini-disasters, and the like force employees to act immediately.

Table 11: Payment Prohibited for Casual, Voluntary and Customary Overtime (by percentage)

377 Companies with Provision	Number	Casual	Voluntary	Customary
		84%	68%	38%
Industry				
Construction......................	20	75	75	25
Manufacturing	226	90	75	44
Utility...........................	48	88	73	50
Banks............................	42	76	48	19
Insurance........................	32	50	34	22
Retail...........................	9	89	67	22

Table 12: Companies Limiting Paid Overtime to Formally Extended Work Schedules (by percentage)

Number of Companies	
All 372 Companies...	23%
224 Manufacturing	25
41 Utilities	12
43 Banks..	21
34 Insurance...	3
22 Construction..	50
8 Retail	37

Awaiting formal management approval of an extended work schedule is not feasible in this industry in most cases. On the other hand, in the construction industry extended schedules are planned into the job and into the bids for the jobs. In this industry the practice is not only feasible, it is part of basic business planning in many, if not most, instances. In the insurance industry, most of the overtime currently is due to special projects problems involving computer personnel. Here, again, while some of the overtime may be planned ahead, much of it is of an emergent nature.

Another method of controlling exempt overtime, employed by a significant percentage of companies, is to limit paid overtime to exempts to periods when nonexempt employees under their supervision are also working. The practice is more prevalent in the manufacturing industries and among retail and construction companies than in banking, insurance and utility companies. The reasons for the differences are probably to be found in the fact that exempts in manufacturing, retail and construction are more likely to have large crews to supervise, while exempts in banking and insurance are more often those professional or technical persons whose work is more of an individual effort. Although utilities also employ many exempts who supervise crews, they nonetheless do not (in the majority) follow the practice of limiting paid overtime to exempts to those times when nonexempts are also working. Table 13 reflects the differences among industries.

Table 13: Companies Limiting Compensable Overtime for Exempt Personnel to Periods When Nonexempt Personnel Are Working (by percentage)

Number of Companies	
All 352 Companies	30%
225 Manufacturing	38
49 Utilities	14
44 Banks	16
19 Construction	21
8 Retail	25
7 Insurance	14

Paid Time Off and Overtime

Since exempt personnel generally receive full pay while taking time off during excused absences for such purposes as vacation, illness, civic duties (jury duty), and urgent approved personal reasons, companies must reach a decision to count such time off as time worked or not when calculating time put in for compensable overtime. The general practice followed for nonexempts may not be a good guide in considering the policy for exempts, since the law does not cover exempt personnel, and most companies follow the provisions of the law strictly in treating the nonexempt situations. Exempt personnel generally receive full pay plus benefits during reasonable and especially approved time off. This is one of the main reasons why a very sizable number of companies do not pay exempts for overtime at all.

Despite this, a majority of the companies surveyed do count vacation, illness and civic duty time off as time worked, as Table 14 shows.

Table 14: Time Off With Pay Counted as Time Worked (by percentage)

Number of Companies	Vacation	Illness	Personal	Civic
203 Manufacturing	62%	62%	48%	60%
52 Banks and Insurance.	37	31	29	33
41 Utilities	64	61	49	61
19 Construction.	53	48	32	58
8 Retail.	25	13	13	13
Total: 323 Companies.	56	55	43	54

Control by Rate Limits

Many companies find that costs of overtime payments to exempt personnel can be further controlled by setting limits on the payments themselves. In some instances instead of paying time-and-one-half for overtime, they pay base rate plus a percentage less than 50 percent (that is, 30 percent). In other instances they pay flat dollar amounts. For example, a bank pays its exempts a flat $40 regardless of their base rates for time spent during Saturday openings of its branch offices.

Other companies limit the total amounts that will be paid for exempt overtime regardless of the hours of work involved. Some limit the total per day, some per week, and some per month. Still others have more complicated formulas, paying one-and-a-half times base up to certain limits, straight time up to higher limits, and zero beyond that.

Chapter 4
Rates of Overtime Pay for Exempt Staff

WHILE NEITHER the Fair Labor Standards Act nor the Walsh-Healey Act apply to the class of employees covered in this survey, they do affect company practices regarding such employees. One of the less obvious facts that emerges from the analysis of the eligibility rules contained in the majority of the plans studied (and to a degree in the other control mechanisms) is the attempt companies make to define the exempt status and the degree of exemption of certain classes of employees.

Wage-hour legislation also influences company decisions about the rates that will be paid to exempt staff. For example, 32 percent of the plans studied provide for legal rate (1.5 times base) for both exempt and nonexempt personnel. Another 16 percent of the plans call for the payment of the 1.5 times base rate up to given levels of salary, then taper the rate downward in steps—sometimes two or more—up to higher levels of salary, and cut it off at levels which are well beyond any question as to exempt status under federal or state law.

One of the congressional intents of the wage-hour laws was to discourage the practice of working employees overtime and to encourage full employment by assessing a penalty on overtime work. The result has been to benefit exempt personnel already employed, since it is far less costly to pay an occasional 50 percent premium than to incur a permanent 100 percent cost.

About one-half of the companies surveyed prefer the simplicity of a straight-time plan for their exempt employees. A few companies make it even simpler by paying a flat dollar rate for overtime worked by exempt staff. But a significant number of companies in the manufacturing industry, among utilities, banks and insurance companies have adopted "formula" plans. These are usually quite sophisticated and are to be found among the larger companies (5,000 employees or more) that generally have the administrative staff to conceive and operate the more complicated type of policy. Moreover, they are more likely to employ a wider variety of classes of exempt staff, making a more sophisticated plan necessary. But there are differences among industries as well. Formula plans have been adopted by significant percentages of companies in the manufacturing (16 percent) and utility companies (17 percent), but they are favored by a much larger percentage of banks and insurance companies (26 percent). However, they are nonexistent among construction and retail companies.

Changing Patterns of Prevalence

Several changing patterns of prevalence have been indicated by the survey data compared with the study conducted in 1967 by The Conference Board. As mentioned before, the sample of companies in this survey is considerably larger, having a marked effect on the statistical results. Also, two industries were added to this survey (retail and construction), clearly affecting the results.

But by eliminating the two added industries, we come fairly close to the sample of the earlier study. Although the comparison is not precise, it is indicative. Among manufacturers, the prevalence of the straight-time plan has dropped 5 percent; among utilities it is off 2 percent and among banks and insurance companies 2 percent. Manufacturers have adopted an increased percentage of plans calling for time-and-one-half (up 13 percent), as have utilities (up 12 percent), banks and insurance companies (up 14 percent). When the two added industries are included, the aggregate change in prevalence is straight-time—off 1 percent; time-and one-half—up 13 percent; formulas—off 17 percent. (See Tables 15 and 16).

Another indication of trend is the preference shown when plans are adopted for the first time by companies. Among manufacturers that have adopted plans since 1974, 65 percent favor the straight-time approach, 28 percent the 1.5 times base approach; and only 7 percent have adopted formula plans. Among nonmanufacturers, 54 percent preferred the straight-time method; 31 percent the 1.5 times base; and 15 percent have elected the formula approach. Table 17 shows the trend over time for manufacturing and nonmanufacturing industries.

Clearly, straight time is favored by the majority of companies that have overtime pay plans for their exempt personnel. But time-and-one-half is growing in favor at the expense of the formula or step plan.

How Formula Plans Work

There is almost no uniformity in the formulas used by the companies that have adopted them. The reason is obvious—the formulas are based on the specific organization structure and salary scales of each company. Indeed, in a few companies that use the Hay System of job evaluation, Hay Points are set as the breaking levels in the formulas.

Table 15: Rates of Overtime Compensation—Daily or Weekly Hours, by Industry

Rates	Manufacturing		Utility		Banks and Insurance		Construction		Retail		All Companies	
	Number	Percent	Number	Percent	Number	Percent	Number	Percent	Number	Percent	Number	Percent
Straight time	84	45%	18	51%	15	36%	13	77%	3	60%	133	47%
Time-and-one-half	60	32	9	26	16	38	4	23	2	40	91	32
Rate determined by a formula	30	16	6	17	11	26	—	—	—	—	47	16
Straight time and/or time-and-a-half, depending on circumstances	13	7	2	6	—	—	—	—	—	—	15	5
Total	187	100%	35	100%	42	100%	17	100%	5	100%	286	100%

Table 16: Types of Formula Plans, by Industry

	Manufacturing		Utility		Banks and Insurance		All Companies	
Regressive scale with two steps	7	23%	2	33%			9	19%
Regressive scale with more than two steps	14	47	3	50	2	18%	19	40
Flat dollar rate	6	20					6	13
Percent of base rate	3	10	1	17	9	82	13	28
	30	100%	6	100%	11	100%	47	100%

Table 17: Rate of Daily-Weekly Overtime Pay, by Date Plan Adopted , by Industry

| | Manufacturing | | | | | | Nonmanufacturing | | | | | |
| | 1X | | 1½X | | Formula | | 1X | | 1½X | | Formula | |
Date Adopted	Number	Percent	Number	Percent	Number	Percent	Number	Percent	Number	Percent	Number	Percent
1974-Present..	35	65%	15	28%	4	7%	33	54%	19	31%	9	15%
1965-1973......	24	45	19	35	11	20	18	56	6	19	8	25
Before 1965....	12	26	19	40	16	34	4	31	6	46	3	23
Total........	71	46%	53	34%	31	20%	55	52%	31	29%	20	19%

Table 17: Rate of Daily-Weekly Overtime Pay, by Date Plan Adopted by Industry (continued)

| | All Companies | | | | | |
| | 1X | | 1½X | | Formula | |
Date Adopted	Number	Percent	Number	Percent	Number	Percent
1974-Present..	68	59%	34	30%	13	11%
1965-1973......	42	49	25	29	19	22
Before 1965....	16	27	25	42	19	32
Total........	126	48%	84	32%	51	20%

Some of the formulas use percentage of base rate in calculating the overtime benefit; others use flat dollar rates per hour, week or month. Some plans are progressive, increasing the benefit as the number of hours of overtime increase. Others are regressive, decreasing the rates of overtime as the salary level increases. Some of these contain two steps, others have three or more. Each type is considered below.

Percent-of-Pay Plans

Percent-of-pay plans are applied in three different ways. One type merely sets rates at, say, base plus 30 percent as the premium for overtime worked by exempt staff. A second type is progressive in application; for example, 15 percent is added to the base rate for less than 8 hours of overtime and 30 percent for hours in excess of 8 hours. The third method is to decrease the percent premium as the salary level of the person working exceeds certain levels; for example, base plus 50 percent for exempts in the $20,000 or lower brackets, base plus 30 percent for salary levels up to $25,000, straight time above that to bonus level managers, and zero above that level.

Flat Dollar Rates

This method of overtime compensation is favored more by banks and insurance companies than by any other industry. One of these plans pays exempt staff $40 for their work in branch offices on Saturday morning openings. Other plans set flat hourly rates to be paid to all exempts alike, regardless of base salary rate. Others set slightly higher flat rates for longer periods of overtime worked, and still others increase the flat rates as salary levels rise, generally in two or more steps.

Regressive Scale, Step Plans

In this type of plan, the overtime premium decreases as the salary level of the exempt overtime worker increases. For example, "time-and-one-half for employees earning up to $1,500 per month; straight time for employees earning between $1,501 and $2,000 per month; zero premium above $3,000."

A variation of this system is to define the break points in terms of salary grades rather than dollars of earnings. This system has the disadvantage of causing inequities. Since salary ranges overlap, a high-paid employee in a lower salary grade may get a higher overtime premium than a low-paid employee in a higher grade. This disadvantage is overcome in some companies by defining the break points in terms of job evaluation "points."

From an examination of the plans surveyed, it appears that many of the regressive "step" plans attempt to escape any possible challenge by wage-and-hour administrative agencies by paying time-and-one half to exempt personnel whose base earnings may not be clearly sufficient to qualify as exempt under the law and to taper the premiums off as the exempt status becomes more clear. The majority of the companies seem to rely more on other criteria. Some of these criteria are:

- Factory first-line supervisors, as opposed to other exempt employees;
- Supervisors whose workers are all nonexempt, as opposed to supervisors of other exempt personnel
- Exempt specialists, as opposed to their supervisors and managers;
- Exempt employees who work on shifts, as opposed to other groups of exempt staff;
- Exempt employees who attain exempt status because they routinely handle confidential administrative duties, as opposed to managers or highly paid professional or technical employees.

Break Points or Limits

The break points or the limits above which no overtime premium will be paid, or no overtime will be compensable, reflect the salary and wage rates in effect in individual companies. Some of the limits are rooted to base hourly rates; others to daily, weekly and monthly rates. The pattern of the data provided in 35 plans permitted the following listings:

Hourly Rates	Daily Rates	Weekly Rates	Monthly Rates
$21.54	$125	$865	$2,580
22.20	120	742.80	675)
19.26	75	478.62 ←	660) ←
16.00	65	250	200
15.33	50	200	
14.00	50 ←		
13.50)	50		
12.75) ←	40		
10.13	35		
10.00	10		
10.00	7		
8.00			
7.50			
4.00			
Base + $2			

Chapter 5
Weekend and Holiday Pay

MUCH OF THE PROBLEM OVERTIME worked by exempt employees consists of weekend work. Indeed, many of the overtime compensation plans had their origin in the solution of compensation questions related to the sixth workday or shift in the normal five-day, forty-hour week.

Many firms pay for work performed on Saturdays, Sundays and holidays regardless of the amount of time put in during the rest of the week. For example, if a factory foreman in such a firm were to work a full eight-hour shift on Sunday, the individual would be credited with eight hours overtime, even if he or she had not reported for work on Wednesday and had put in only thirty-two normal hours of work that week, plus the eight hours on Sunday (assuming the absence was excused). Most firms, however, do require that an exempt employee must have first put in the normal 40 hours during the week to qualify for overtime pay.

Most firms require that the employee's work schedule be formally extended to include the weekend work. The most common reasons for the extension are inventory taking, year-end closing for accounting personnel, or seasonal demand on production staff.

Pay Patterns

The vast majority of all 443 firms surveyed (almost three-fourths) make no distinction between Saturday, Sunday or holidays in the rates or amounts they pay exempt personnel for overtime work performed on those days. But a significant number do, equating holiday work at a considerably higher premium than normal overtime or Saturday and Sunday.

The plans of 148 firms provided sufficient information to derive the patterns of pay for weekend and holiday pay. In that group of firms there are 26 different combinations of pay policies for Saturday as against Sunday and holiday work.

The largest number of firms in the group (48) pay straight time for all three days not normally considered workdays. The next most frequently found pattern is time-and-one-half for all three days (35). The next most common pattern (21) is time-and-one-half for Saturday and double time for Sundays and holidays. Together, these three patterns comprise 70 percent of all 148 plans. The remaining 30 percent range from no pay on Saturday to triple time on holidays; some giving flat rates that vary and others flat rates that remain the same for each type of weekend day.

Table 18 indicates the combinations of rates that are provided in each of the 148 plans studied.

Table 18: Weekend and Holiday Overtime Rates for Exempt Employees in 148 Companies

Saturday	Sunday	Holiday	Number of Companies
1X	1X	1X	48
1.5X	1.5X	1.5X	35
1.5X	2X	2X	21
Flat Rate*	Flat Rate*	Flat Rate*	6
1X	1X	2X	5
1.5X	2X	2.5X	5
1.5	2X	1.5X	4
1.5X	1.5X	2.5X	3
1X	1X	2X	2
1X	1.5X	1.5X	2
Gradual Scale beginning with 1½ X for all three days			1
1.5X	1.5X	2X	1
$ 45 per day for all three days			1
$ 10 per hour for all three days			1
$ 65 per day for all three days			1
$ 30 per day for all three days			1
$ 25 per day for all three days			1
$ 4 per hour for all three days			1
$120 per day	120 per day	$155 per day	1
$ 12 per day	$ 16 per hour	$ 16 per hour	1
$2X	2X	2X	1
1.5X	2X	3X	1
Zero	1.46X	2X	1
1.62X	2.16X	2.16X	1
Zero	1.06X monthly rate	Zero	1
$60 per day	$120 per day	Zero	1
Zero	1.25X	1.5X	1
			148

Report No.